RE Ideas: Sacred Places

Most people have a place or a series of places that are significant to them because of events, memories, experiences or the people that they encounter there. This publication makes the bridge between these significant places and places that people consider to be sacred.

All religions have places that are considered sacred, and this book focuses on places of worship as sacred, but also on the nature and evidence of religion in the local community. Later books in the series will focus on spiritual development and journey and will include units on other sacred places. This book supports pupils in learning about the significance of places of worship to those who belong and also to the communities that they serve. The units move beyond the simple naming and learning of technical vocabulary to focus on aspects of the sacred place which reflect beliefs and values important to particular religious communities.

The book provides an excellent resource in the form of large cutaway pictures of a church and a mosque including a series of strategies to allow these to be used across the age range. With our youngest children we begin by exploring what sacred means in nature, in a stained glass window, and in the whole world. A series of practical units support learning, including one on creating a school sacred place, a cross-curricular unit on 'religion in your community' and a dilemma for older pupils on 'should we sell the church?' Many of the units have been written so that the strategies can be adapted depending on the sacred places you are studying. The units encourage enquiry learning, creative engagement and children's own questions and reflections. For the subject leader we also provide further guidance on visiting places of worship – such as what to wear and dealing with parental concerns – and one of our ever-popular progression grids.

Fiona Moss
Editor

Support material on the RE Today website

The RE Today website offers subscribers some free additional resources and classroom-ready materials related to this publication. Look out for the 'RE Today on the web' logo at the end of selected articles.

The password for access can be found in each term's *REtoday* magazine or you can use your subscriber number.

What is a sacred place?

Background knowledge for teachers

This set of learning ideas will enable pupils aged 4–6 to enjoy learning about sacred places. There are four examples: for some people, trees are holy places; for Jewish people, a sukkah is one kind of sacred place; a Christian might say a stained glass window in a church is sacred; some people say the whole world is sacred. On completion, children will be asked to think about the different ideas of holy or sacred spaces they have learned about, and say what each one means.

Sacred trees: In the Jewish Bible stories of Abraham, a tree is often the place where God is heard, or sensed. In many other traditions, trees are sacred because they are mighty, long lived, beyond our making, giving us shelter, fruit, branches, leaves or wood to use in building. Learning about a tree opens up excellent connections from RE and art to history and understanding the world. Personal development work for children can be smoothly linked to finding out about trees.

Jewish festival: Sukkot In memory of the 40 years that their ancestors wandered the deserts of Sinai after escaping from Egyptian slavery, Jewish people camp out in a temporary shelter once a year for eight days. The family builds a sukkah, with temporary walls and a leafy roof, and eat their meals outdoors. Some people – and children often love this – might also sleep in the sukkah. It makes you realise what it might have been like for the wandering ex-slaves in the desert, even if you can go in to use the bathroom!

A Christian church: put what matters in the window Many Christian churches celebrate an aspect of their faith in stained glass. Images of Christ, crosses, the holy family, the stories of scripture or saints and angels, bread and wine are common.

The whole earth is sacred – what does that mean? After finding out about trees, Jewish temporary shelters and Christian windows, children have a think about a big idea, that the whole of our planet is sacred. This is not an alternative to religious kinds of sacredness: many Jewish and Christian people, for example, try to love the earth and care for the planet because they see it as God's gift to humanity.

Assessment for Learning

This section shows some of the outcomes achievable by pupils of different abilities in the 4–6 age range.

Level	Description of achievement: I can ...
1 Almost all pupils in this age group	• listen to a story from a religion • notice an example of a religious object or word • *talk about my feelings in relation to a story* • *be aware of different cultures and beliefs.*
2 Many pupils in this age group	• recall the outline of a religious story • name a holy building for Christians and for Jews • *talk about a symbol, and about what makes a place feel special* • identify two different religions
3 The most able pupils in this age group	• retell the story of Moses and the Burning Bush • suggest some meanings for the story • *respond to ideas about God in the stories and festivals* • *respond sensitively to questions about places special or sacred to me.*

This unit helps pupils in Scotland to achieve RME 1-04b.

Essential pupil knowledge

Pupils should:

• know that 'sacred' or 'holy' are words that describe a religious kind of 'special' and be able to use the words
• know religions are both similar to each other and different from each other.
• be able to think and speak for themselves about simple religious or spiritual questions.

W Web support

http://tinyurl.com/nuve9ts is a good introductory animation. RE Today subscribers can download:
• outlines for the drawings on p.3
• an outline of the tryptych on p.5
• the Earth picture on p.7.

RE Today Services

Activity 1 — Trees

Ask the pupils to think of all the parts of a tree they can. Aim for roots, trunk, branches, bark, twigs, leaves, fruits, at least. Next add some things that some trees have, but not all trees have, for example, needles, conkers, flowers, apples.

Now ask the pupils to imagine a world with no trees: we would be short of lots of other things too. No apples, pears, plums. No nuts or palm leaves, nothing made out of wood. No rubber, no shade, no conkers or falling leaves in autumn. No Christmas trees. No woods and no forests. Nowhere for birds to sit and sing or squirrels to run. What else?

Ask the pupils if they think it is a good idea to love, care for and protect our trees. Tell them that trees are special in many ways, and some people use a religious word for special – it is 'sacred'. Another word that means the same thing is 'holy'.

Show the children the animation about the Genesis Creation story (from the web resource box on p.2), and ask them to remember and list all the animals and birds they recognised. Tell them that Jewish and many Christian people believe God made trees (along with everything else). So a tree can be sacred.

Leaf display

Ask pupils to take two leaf outlines like those below, one green and one orange. In the green leaf, draw something that they like to see growing. In the brown one, something that should be shrinking. Talk about the task and make a display of a spring tree and an autumn tree out of the pupils' leaves.

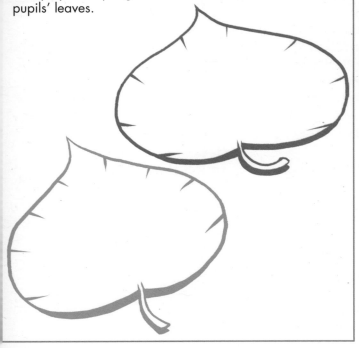

Activity 2 — Moses and Burning Bush

Tell this story to the class – it comes from Exodus chapter 6 in the Jewish Bible. Ask if the children have heard any stories of Moses before, and tell them he was one of the great leaders who started the Jewish religion.

> Moses had hoped he might be a great leader for his people, who were all slaves in Egypt, but that was before he lost his temper and killed a man. He ran away into the desert. For years, all he did was look after a flock of sheep. One day in the desert he saw a bush, a little tree, on fire. But it wasn't burning up. He went closer. Then he heard a mysterious voice: 'Moses, I am the God of your fathers. Take your shoes off. This ground is holy. I will send you to set my people free.' Moses took off his shoes. He was amazed by the bush, but even more by the voice. After many worries, he went back to Egypt to deal with the evil Pharaoh, and lead God's people to freedom.

Tell the class that this story of the burning bush is always remembered in the Jewish religion. If you are lucky enough to have a forest school area at your school, then you could tell the story, then burn a bush in your fire pit while observing all health and safety requirements.

Give pupils a red flame outline, and ask them to draw into the outline an amazed face for Moses. Make a burning bush display out of the flame shapes.

Ask the class 'Who has slept in a tent?' and talk about why it is sometimes exciting. Tell the children that in the next part of the story of Moses, he and the slaves escaped from Egypt and the evil Pharaoh, and made a new life living in the desert and travelling from place to place. They lived in tents. They lived like this for years. Even though this happened about 3400 years ago, the Jewish people still remember it with a festival today. Can they guess what happens? Ask talking partners to make three guesses each, and share them with others.

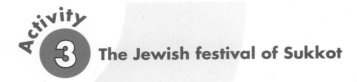

Activity 3 — The Jewish festival of Sukkot

Making dens

Through role play pupils can explore relationships, cultures, faiths and attitudes, key themes in RE. By playing collaboratively and co-operatively, with expert adult interaction, pupils will develop respect, a set of values and communication skills. This activity is a lot of fun, and if it is linked carefully to stories about Jewish life and celebration, it enables deepening RE learning. Here is a practical idea for play-based RE.

In a team, make a den!

Ask pupils in teams of six or more if they think they could make a den, like a sukkah – the shelter Jewish people use to remember the times long ago when their ancestors lived in tents in the desert. Tell them that a sukkah has a natural roof, made of leaves or branches, and the side walls are never complete – they included gaps, to keep the air flowing through! You have to be able to see the stars from inside the sukkah, so don't make the roof too complete. Jewish people often decorate the sukkah with fake fruits – make these from card or paper if you like. How many different paper fruits

can the pupils include? Pupils can explore natural materials and construction through the building of sukkahs. Learning through playing is all about experimentation, making connections, negotiating with others, discussion and questioning. Encourage this kind of approach.

Some pupils (or your whole class?) might prefer to make their sukkah like a doll's house, for 'small world' people, but there is fun to be had doing this to a big scale, in the open air. A sheet or other piece of fabric for each team might be helpful, and pupils can use whatever is to hand, learning of course how to do this safely as they go. Tell the pupils that you – or another adult – will be 'Moses' at the end of the den-making and come round to visit all the different sukkah, telling them a bit more of the story. Hot-seat yourself, and invite their questions. Can pupils eat their lunch, or a break-time snack in the sukkah? Can they taste some Jewish foods?

Activity 4 — Being thankful

Show pupils two special things from the festival of Sukkot if you can: the *etrog* is like a huge lemon, and the *lulav* is a kind of bunch of reeds. Tell them that Jewish people like to thank God for their homes, for their freedom and for their food. Demonstrate the way Jewish people hold and wave the etrog and the lulav, as they give thanks to the Almighty: 'Blessed are You, Lord our God, King of the Universe, you who have blessed us with your commandments.'
Clip 3577 from the BBC Learning Zone is potentially useful for six-year-olds: www.bbc.co.uk/learningzone/clips/
Talk about these symbols and actions.

What makes you thankful? Ask the pupils in each den team to make up a chant of things they are grateful for, and perform it for the rest of the class:

> For fish and chips
> Thanks very much
> For mums and dads
> Thanks very much
> For sun and rain
> Thanks very much
> For family and friends…

Can they choose ten things of their own to be thankful for?

RE Today
Services

Activity 5

What matters? Put it in the window – Christian churches and stained glass

Remember and reflect

Remind the pupils that, for Jewish people, a Sukkah could be a sacred space. For Moses, a tree that burned was a holy place. Ask them some reminder and reflection questions about the earlier lessons. Tell them that in this lesson we will find out about one way some Christian people make a church feel special or sacred.

Stained glass

Ask pupils if they know about stained glass windows. Do any pupils have coloured glass in their windows at home? When the sun shines through, it can be beautiful. Some examples from the internet will get them talking – you might choose four examples, and explore them, and then ask pupils to say which is their favourite and why.

Make your own

Give pupils a 10cm square of dark sugar paper to fold and cut into, so that they make a pattern of cut-outs. Demonstrate how a pattern can be made with a few very small cuts (this makes a useful link to ELGs for Mathematics). Stick a sheet of coloured cellophane behind the sugar paper. If all the pupils do this, you can make a large stained glass window by sticking them all to a window. Can a small group of pupils devise a nice arrangement, for example a cross, or colour matched?

What do Christians put in their stained glass windows?

An internet search of 100 stained glass windows to see which images are most popular yielded 15 pictures of Jesus back from the dead, 12 of Jesus being crucified, 8 of Jesus in the manger, 4 of the story of Noah and 3 each of angels, a tree and a river. Ask pupils to guess which were most popular. Talk about why these images are found most often in the stained glass windows in churches. Is it because these are the things that matter to Christians? Is that the same as saying these things are holy or sacred for Christians?

A whole class triptych

Tell the pupils that they are going to make a whole class triptych – it is a work of art with three panels in it. Use the template below, blown up tenfold, or draw one onto three sheets of A0 sized paper. Each child is asked to make three drawings with a bright border around them.

- The first one, with a purple border, is a drawing of something that matters very much to them.
- The second one, with a yellow border, is to be something that matters to a friend (they might do this in pairs, and should talk about it).
- The third one is to be something they have found out that matters to Christians. Give it a bright red border. Collect all the images, and give a small group – with a TA to support them – the task of arranging, trimming and then sticking them to the triptych outline to make a work of art that shows what matters to the children and to Christians. You might use the finished product to talk about in assembly, or to present to a local Christian community. If you stick it onto large pieces of cardboard, it can stand alone – as triptychs were designed to do originally.

What matters to me? What matters to you? What matters to Christians?

Activity 6a Is the whole earth sacred? Using a Jewish song

Tell the pupils that lots of people think the world, the earth, is sacred or holy. They will be able to think about this idea, and make some choices. They will hear two songs, one Jewish and one Christian, that say the world is a holy place because God made it. Jews and Christians are two different religions – but they agree about this.

Play the pupils a Jewish song about Creation:

http://tinyurl.com/qgthd9m

Put some flash cards on the floor in circle time, and ask the pupils if they can put them in the right order from the song: light/day/night/earth/seas/flowers/grass/fruit trees/moon/stars/sun/birds/fish/animals/humans.

They may need to hear the song two or three times to get them all in the right order. You could talk about songs from around the world and in different languages – do any children want to sing one? This song is partly in Hebrew, the language of the Jews, but lots in English too. After this, ask the children: of all the things on the cards, which are their three favourites? Why? Talking partners can discuss this.

Activity 7 Is the whole earth sacred?

On p.7 there is a design template to get pupils to create a collage of their own favourite things about the earth, responding to the question 'Is the whole earth sacred?'

Ask pupils to

- collage or colour the land and the sea
- choose five or more favourite things on the whole planet to draw in the blue circle, or use cut-out pictures
- choose three words to put onto the world. You could offer the pupils a selection of words to choose from: **holy/sacred/special/beautiful/God's gift/ precious/lovely/wonderful**
- cut out the world.

Once you have all the class's collages you can create a hanging display.

Activity 6b Is the whole earth sacred? Using a Christian song

'Wonderful World' by Stephen Fischbacher is a Christian song about Creation.

Ask pupils 'What is your favourite … ?'

- view
- mountain, lake, place in the world
- fish, wild animal, insect, bird
- domestic animal (pet)
- part of the body
- weather
- flower
- country.

Collect some answers, which you can turn into a list poem, making another verse of this song.

**Angel Falls, Everest,
Grand Canyon, Loch Ness
Sahara Desert, too hot for me,
Float in the waters of the Dead Sea.**

**Isn't it just a wonderful world,
A wonderful world that we live in?
And whoever made this wonderful world
Is someone that I can believe in.**

**Beehive, honeycomb, racing pigeon, flying home
Platypus, kangaroo, in the wild and in the zoo
Heart beating, like a drum, fingerprint, on my thumb
Heads, shoulder, knees and toes, I think that's how the song goes.**

**Snowflakes drift down, lightning strikes the ground,
Wind whistling through the trees,
Tiny veins on all the leaves.
Africa, India, Scotland, don't forget –
Hot and sunny, freezing cold, huh! Wet!**

Get the pupils to listen to and/or sing the song (from 'Something Fischy', available from RE Today, or via Fischy Music's website: www.fischy.co.uk.

Use this song to explore and raise questions about the wonders of the world and the idea of Creation.

Ask pupils

- what do you think the singer believes?
- how can you tell?

Play the music, and give the pupils the lyrics to see. Ask them if they can, while listening, write down the questions that come into their minds – give them a template to do this.

Ask pupils to make their own 'list poem' of some of the things that amaze them about the world.

The two songs both show how and why some religious people, Jewish or Christian, think the whole world is a holy place, a sacred place.

RE Today
Services

holy	**beautiful**	**precious**
sacred	**God's gift**	**lovely**
special		**wonderful**

What makes somewhere sacred?

Background knowledge for teachers

This unit allows flexibility over the sacred places that you focus on and is therefore suitable for teachers in all schools. We have provided information here about the four most commonly studied places of worship.

Christian holy places include many kinds of church and chapel, where believers worship. These places are used in many denominations for the eucharist, ceremonies and celebrations such as weddings and baptism, and community activities such as children's groups, prayer meetings and social outreach.

For Muslims, a mosque or masjid is a place to prostrate, to bow and submit to Allah, to God – a place of prayer. A Muslim may pray at the mosque, and Friday prayers are usually the biggest occasion for communal prayer. The five daily prayers can be made anywhere, and a prayer mat, facing in the direction of Makkah, is a clean place from which to pray. The mosque is a place of learning, particularly for children.

Hindu worship is often in the home, among the family. There are also numerous mandirs in the UK today, often in urban settings. The deities of Hindu dharma are many; often, a shrine in the home will have a murti (image) of one of the gods or goddesses. Home worship may include singing and prayer by one or more family members. Mandirs install murtis of a number of different deities, and the daily arti, worship, ceremonies, bringing peace, harmony, strength by which to live.

Jewish worship takes place in a synagogue, a Jewish house of worship. It is also called a shul in Yiddish. The synagogue has an ark holding the Torah scrolls. Jews attend synagogue for prayer service at festivals and Shabbat. The synagogue is often a place for Jewish social gatherings, as it is the centre of the local Jewish community. Hebrew school is typically available at synagogues, as are conversion classes.

This unit of work allows pupils to explore a place of worship and understand the concept of sacredness. There is a clear purpose and audience to pupils' learning as they recreate a place of worship and act as tour guides. There are good opportunities for Learning Outside the Classroom as the culmination of this unit is the creation of a school sacred space.

Essential knowledge for pupils

Pupils should know

- The difference between describing a place as special and using the word sacred
- The names and key features and functions of the one or two places of worship studied in this unit.

Assessment for Learning

This section shows some of the outcomes achievable by pupils of different abilities in the 5–7 age range.

Level	Description of achievement: I can ...
1 Almost all pupils in this age group	• **name** a place of worship from a picture and recognise some of the features of it • **talk about** a place that is special for me and why it is special, and talk about what is sacred in a particular place of worship.
2 Many pupils in this age group	• **suggest two reasons** why a person belonging to a particular religion chooses to go to their place of worship • **identify** three **significant features** of a place of worship, matching them to a religion, and suggesting what they are 'used' for • **recognise and share ideas** about the difference between my special place and a sacred place.
3 The most able pupils in this age group	• **give two ways two different places of worship** are **similar** and two ways they are **different** • **suggest some things** that people do to find peace, stillness and rest, including some things I do and suggest why they might do them.

This unit helps pupils in Scotland to achieve RME 1-03a, 1-04b and 1-06a.

Web support

The websites below offer advice on places of worship visits and virtual visits.

REonline
See: www.reonline.org.uk/specials/places-of-worship/
REQuest: Christian places of worship
See: www.request.org.uk
Learning outside the classroom
See: www.lotc.org.uk/what-is-lotc/where-lotc/sacred-spaces/

The following resources are available for download by RE Today subscribers

- A film showing 6-year-olds as tour guides (p.10)
- A visit sheet (p.11).

RE Today
Services

Activity 1 — A special place for you

Share with your pupils the comments from the pupils below. As you read them out, you could miss out the place and see if the pupils can guess which places the pupils are talking about.

> I go to the buddy bench because someone always comes to see if you are all right.
>
> *Iona, aged 6*

> No one can find us when we are behind the greenhouse … we can do quiet things there.
>
> *James, aged 6*

> At home I love to hide under the bed because it is quiet and I can think … I go there when I have been shouted at by mummy.
>
> *Lucy, aged 6*

Ask the pupils to write about or draw a place that is special and significant to them. Discuss what makes these places so important to the pupils. What similarities and differences are there between the places that the pupils have chosen? Agree as a group what the characteristics of a special place are.

Do the pupils know places that are special to some religious people? Can they name any?

Explain that some people think places of worship are much more than special and use the word 'sacred' to describe them. Discuss with the class what might make somewhere a sacred place.

Activity 2 — Why are some places sacred?

Split the pupils into groups of three and give each group either the cutaway picture of the church from p.16 or the cutaway picture of the mosque from p.17.

Ask the pupils to

- Identify any parts of the picture that they can name or explain what is happening.
- Choose three parts of the picture that might make the place sacred. Label them and talk about why some people would say they are sacred.
- Meet up with a group who were looking at the other picture. Discuss what is similar or different about the pictures. Is it similar or different things that make these places sacred for some people?

Activity 3 — Visit to a sacred place

We are far more likely to learn through experiencing something than merely being told it. This is the reason that if at all possible pupils between the ages of 5 and 7 should have the opportunity to visit at least one sacred place.

During this visit pupils will have the opportunity to listen to someone explaining why this place is sacred to the people that belong there. However, pupils should also have the opportunity to record their learning and ideas in an open-ended manner.

The recording sheet on p.11 allows pupils to record the things that they have learnt from or are most interested in learning more about.

When you return to the classroom and discuss the learning, pupils could split into groups to find out more about aspects of the place you visited.

If for some reason it is absolutely impossible to visit a sacred place or you would like to 'visit' a sacred place that is geographically difficult to access, the website below offers links to virtual visits and other advice about preparing to visit a sacred place.

See: www.reonline.org.uk/specials/places-of-worship/

See: www.request.org.uk

Activity 4 — Sacred space tour guides

For pupils, a purpose and an audience for their learning ignites creativity and enthusiasm. Set your pupils a challenge: explain that another class in the school have been unable to visit the place of worship that you visited and so it is their job to recreate the experience for them.

Ask the pupils to suggest in pairs how this might be achieved. Hopefully, within the suggestions offered, you will receive something similar to the suggestion below. If not, you may want to introduce the activity outlined below or follow the pupils' suggestions – they might be better!

For this activity you need a large space; if weather permits, the playground is ideal.

- Choose a team of four pupils to be the architects for the place of worship.
- The architects then physically move each of the other class members to create the building or significant part of the building outline.
- Once the outline has been created, use masking tape or chalk to draw around the outline. The pupils can now step back and admire the parameters of the place they have recreated.
- Ask the children to work in groups to identify key features in the place of worship.
- These features can then be simply added by a pupil with a label or action representing the item, e.g. font – arms creating a bowl shape; clock – arms as clocks hands, ticking sound. These could also be represented by pupils holding photographs or pictures they have drawn.
- Pupils then rehearse their role as a tour guide. They practise what they will say at various parts of the tour, how they will describe why significant features are important to believers, and practise answering questions.
- Invite the visitors! This will obviously happen over an extended period, giving as many of the pupils as possible the opportunity to be tour guides.

 Subscribers can watch a video of this lesson in action.

Activity 5 — A sacred space or reflection space for your school

This unit began with the pupils identifying special places around their school and home and then noticing the difference between special and sacred. The final creative class task is to create a sacred or reflection space for your school. This space needs to be suitable for those without religious beliefs and those who hold different religious beliefs. It could be constructed inside or outside. Many are constructed in an enclosed garden or willow structure, with others choosing a corner of an internal corridor. Once a suitable space has been identified you are ready to begin.

Ask the pupils to identify what areas a sacred place often has, and allow them to make suggestions, but you might settle on:

- Reflection space
- Question space
- Community space
- Learning space
- Creative space

Arrange pupils into groups to design each of these areas, considering what they will need to make or collect. Use the photographs on p.12 as a stimulus for the pupils: what makes these spaces sacred? What ideas can the children use from these places?

The final step is to create the sacred space or reflection area. How will it be looked after? When can it be used? Are there any rules that need to be written?

More able pupils can consider what the difference is between their space and a place of worship.

Ask pupils to draw or write about:

- The most important part of our space is ... because ...
- My favourite part of our space is ... because ...
- A Christian/Muslim [etc] might like/not like our space because ...

Jumping Fish produce several publications that support creating areas for reflection or sacred spaces in school.
See: http://gloucester.anglican.org/parish-life/jumping -fish/#ROV

RE Today Services

See 👁	Hear 👂	Smell 👃

Touch ✋	Surprised 😮	Liked 🙂

Most interesting !	My question (s) ?	Sacred 🙏

Photocopiable by purchasing institutions

RE Today
Services

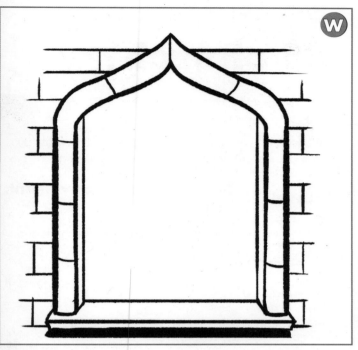

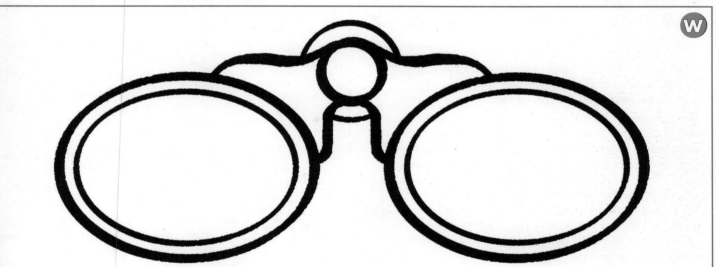

Similarity and difference

If you have looked at sacred places from more than one religion, this activity could allow pupils to compare the sacred places, highlighting similarities and differences. All pupils should be able to compare one sacred place to the school sacred place.

Give pupils a choice of outlines from the three above, they can use one outline or more than one outline depending on the activity. Ask them to:

- Draw what could be happening in the sacred space on a particular day. Ask pupils to annotate their picture and more able pupils could write a description of what is happening.

- Next choose another outline, draw what would be happening in a different sacred space. This could be your school sacred space or a sacred space from a different religion. Ask pupils to annotate their picture and more able pupils could write a description of what is happening. Now they have drawn two they can discuss orally or write similarities and differences between the two places.

- Finally choose another outline and draw what they might like to do to find peace, stillness or rest in either the school sacred place or another place important to them.

What happens in the mosque?
What happens in the church?

Background knowledge for teachers

This section contains resources for use with 7–11s. It offers a way of helping pupils to explore some basic information about two places of worship, but also to go beyond the labelling to think about the significance for believers.

While mosques and churches are important to believers, their significance varies. Many Christians emphasise that the 'Church' is really the community of Christian believers, who are called the 'body' of Christ. Buildings are places to allow Christians to gather together to worship, and to give them a place from which to serve the community. Some newer Protestant church groups use other buildings, such as school halls. The Holy Qur'an says that 'The world, the whole of it, is a Mosque [a place of prayer] … Wherever you turn, there is the face of God' (2:115). The mosque itself reveals some key Muslim beliefs, such as the idea of ummah or community, submission, and the Oneness of God.

Two wonderful illustrations offer cutaway images of a church and a mosque. The church is a Baptist church, to offer a contrast with Anglican and Roman Catholic churches. Many Protestant churches have a similar layout, with prominence given to the pulpit for preaching the Bible as the Word of God, although not all will have a baptistry pool for baptism by full immersion. The activities also make connections with the lives of pupils by focusing on ideas such as peace, service and purpose.

Essential knowledge for pupils

Pupils should know:

- that mosques and churches are important to believers but that their significance and use varies
- some key beliefs of Christianity shown in the church such as following the word of God, worship, prayer and community
- some key Muslim beliefs, such as the idea of ummah or community, submission, and the Oneness of God.

Assessment for Learning

This section shows some of the outcomes achievable by pupils of different abilities in the 7–11 age range.

Level	Description of achievement: I can …
2 Almost all pupils in this age group	• **name** some parts of a church and mosque • *talk about* how people might feel in a place of worship, including myself.
3 Many pupils in this age group	• **use the correct vocabulary** for different parts of a church and mosque, and say some things that are the **same** and some things that are **different** between them • *ask some good questions* about why worshippers go to church or mosque.
4 Many pupils in this age group	• **show that I understand** why places of worship can be important to Christians and Muslims, making links between these two traditions • *refer to two places of worship to* **show that I understand** how they express what matters to Christians and Muslims.
5 The most able pupils in this age group	• **explain how** worshipping in a church or mosque can affect the lives of believers and communities • *relate the idea that* God may be encountered/heard/felt in the worship in church or mosque with my own ideas about music, stillness, prayer, peace, service **and community reflection.**

This unit helps pupils in Scotland to achieve RME 1-01b, 1-04a, 1-04b, 2-03a, 2-04c and 2-06a.

Web support

The following resources are available for download by RE Today subscribers:
- The pictures of the mosque and church on pp.16–17.

RE Today Services

Different strategies can be used with pupils of different abilities and ages. Choose strategies which relate to the learning outcomes you have selected for your pupils.

Listing and labelling

Here are 24 words linked with a church, a mosque, or both. You might introduce them to the class first and then give pupils the labels to put onto the picture in the right place; or you might give pupils the pictures and a dictionary, and get them to work out for themselves the correct places. Get them to practise saying and writing the words.

minbar	youth group	madrassah
qibla wall	dome	Sunday school
washroom	balcony	clocks
prayer	prayer mats	kitchen
Jesus	worship	mihrab
pastor	imam	library
shoe rack	God	minaret
baptistry	pulpit	worship band

Spot the difference

Ask pupils to find at least five similarities and five differences between the two places of worship.

- Why do they think there are some things that are the same and some that are different between a Christian and a Muslim place of worship?

Framing: what matters most?

1 Give pupils a small cardboard or paper frame and ask them to place it on the picture over the place that they think is: busiest, happiest, noisiest, most important, most holy. There are no specific right answers, so pupils should give good reasons for their choices.

2 Where do pupils think that worshippers will find peace and why? Where do worshippers learn most, and why? Where do worshippers get a chance to serve others? Where is the place for the youngest, and for the oldest? Where is there somewhere for all ages together? Where do worshippers go to find a purpose for their lives? Where do worshippers get most help with their lives, when they are struggling?

3 Follow this up with some reflection on pupils' own lives. Where do they find peace, and why? Where do they learn most, and why? Where do they get a chance to serve others? Where do they go where people of all ages go together? How do they decide the purpose in their own lives? Where do they get most help when they are struggling? Talk about how and why their own answers are similar and different to the answers from (1).

Maps from memory

Get pupils to work in groups of four. Their aim is to accurately recreate the picture you are showing them. To succeed, the pupils must use technical vocabulary to help the team.

Pupil 1 from each group comes to the front of the class and you show them one of the pictures for ten seconds. They go back to their groups and explain to Pupil 2 what they saw, and Pupil 2 draws according to their direction. After two minutes, all the Pupil 2s have a ten-second look at the picture and explain what they have seen for Pupil 3 to draw.

Go around twice and then get pupils to show other groups their drawings, explaining what they have drawn. Show them the real image and get them to give the pictures marks out of ten for accuracy!

Alien report

Imagine that you are aliens of high intelligence who are on a mission to find out about life on earth. Your spaceship lands near a large building. Using your x-ray vision you look through the walls and see the scene on pp.16–17. You know nothing about what human beings do. What do you think is happening? What might be going on? Working in groups, write your report. What might the creatures be doing in this place?

Read some of your alien reports. Did your reports get it right? Could you tell what and why the human beings are behaving like this? Why not? What would you need to do to find out what is actually going on and why? Being able to speak with the human beings, asking questions, spending more time observing, reading the religious stories and teachings – all of these will help the aliens to be able to get their report right. Use this approach to start an investigation into what it means to be a Christian or Muslim and to worship God.

A good follow-up to this strategy is 'Alien questions' on p.18.

Tour guide

Ask pupils to imagine they are part of the welcome team for the church or mosque. They have a group of children aged 7–8 coming on a visit. To which three parts of the church or mosque would they take their visitors, and what would they say?

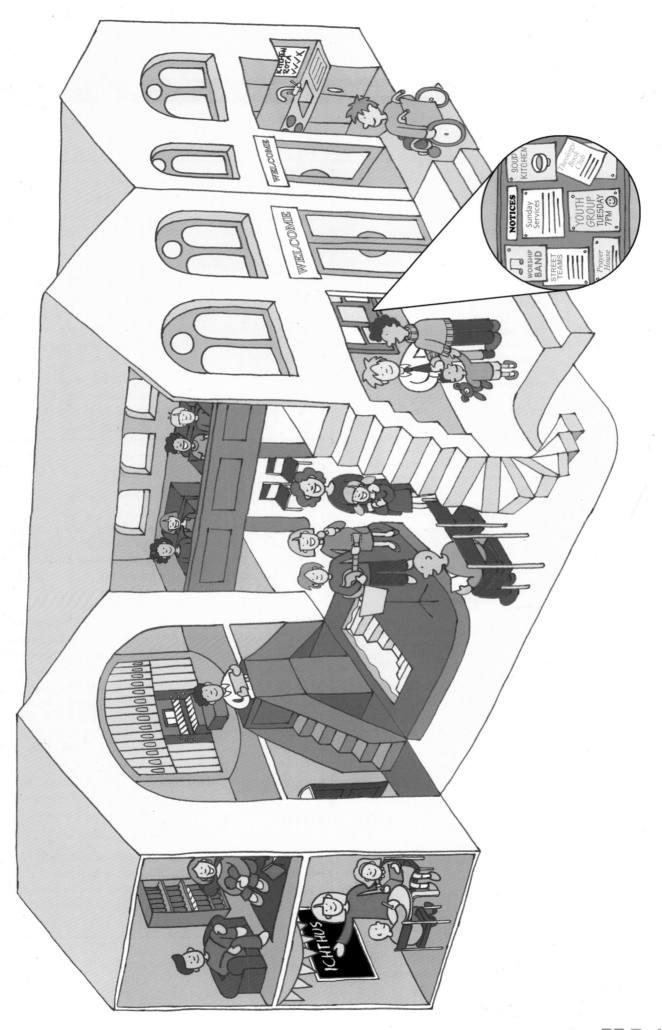

Photocopiable by purchasing institutions

RE Today Services

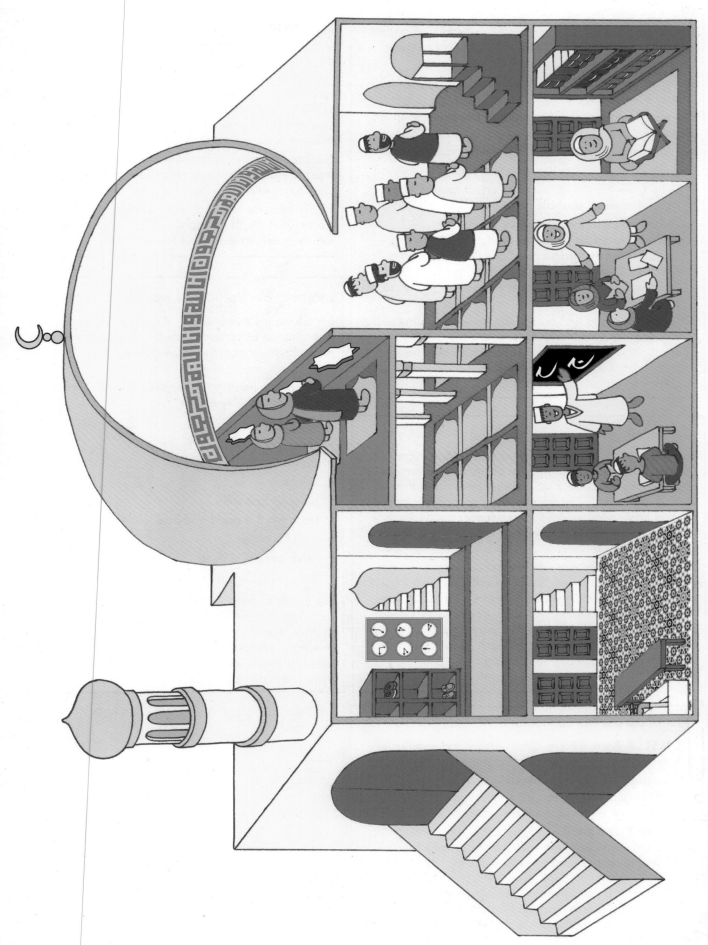

RE Today
Services Photocopiable by purchasing institutions

Alien questions

Having (probably!) got their first Alien Report wrong, set your alien pupils the task of finding out better answers. Start with all the questions pupils can think of.

Question stems are a good place to start: Who/what/where/when/how/why?

Get pupils to direct their questions at three people in the picture.

Go through the questions and sort them into categories.

- Simple categories are Big Questions and Little Questions.
- Others are those with just one correct answer and those with many possible answers.
- These can be further broken down into **comprehension** questions (about understanding the facts); **knowledge** questions (that need some specialist knowledge); **speculation** questions (that use our imagination); and **enquiry** questions (that take us on a journey of discovery).
- Use resources to find out the answers to as many of the questions as possible. Decide on a class enquiry question. Go on a visit or two to places of worship; invite some Christians and Muslims in to answer questions.

Sense trail

Ask pupils to focus on one of their senses. You might get them all to focus on hearing, first of all, or give groups of pupils one sense each. (Smell and taste are the most difficult, of course!) Get them to imagine walking into the building. What would they see/hear/touch? As they wander around the building, what are the key things that strike their senses?

You might do this as a guided reflection, where you get pupils to close their eyes as you describe walking into and around the buildings in the pictures. Or pupils have a copy of one picture and label it with the sounds they might hear (worship music, call to prayer, sermon) or the sensations from what they might touch (shaking hands, washing hands, face and feet, touching the prayer carpet).

Links across the curriculum

SMSC: Reflection on ideas of identity and community, love and service, and to develop sensitivity and respect.

Literacy: Developing skills in spoken language, reading and writing, including questioning, giving reasons and writing for different purposes.

Art and design: Extend the activities by getting pupils to consider ways in which calligraphy and geometric art are used to express the beauty of God in Islam, without trying to draw pictures of God – an activity that is forbidden in Islam, of course. You might ask pupils to create models of different types of church, or specific local or famous mosques.

Meet the people

Introduce Fred, Naomi and Tim from the church and Wasim, Imran and Nasima. Choose people to represent them from the pictures. Six short accounts from these people who use the church or mosque regularly can be found on p.19. Before reading the information, ask pupils to think what they expect these people from the mosque or church to say about what they do and why church/mosque is so important to them.

Next read the verses from the Bible and the Qur'an. Use these to add to their ideas about the importance of the church/mosque.

Finally read the information from the six believers; talk about what pupils got right, what surprised them, and any further questions they would want to ask.

Learning from places of worship

For Christians and Muslims, the places of worship represent an attitude towards God – one of thanksgiving and submission; but they also offer places of community too.

Ask pupils to find out and explain how the place of worship helps believers to:

- say thank you
- say sorry
- praise God
- celebrate
- be quiet and still
- learn what is good and bad
- care for others
- serve people in need
- learn from each other

Ask pupils to consider whether there are any parts of their own lives that are similar or different: where and when do they: say thank you, say sorry, praise [God or …?], celebrate, be quiet and still, learn what is good and bad, care for others, serve people in need, learn from others? Why are these good things to do?

Photocopiable by purchasing institutions

RE Today Services

Learning from six people from the church and mosque (W)

Hello. I'm Fred and I'm one of the welcome team at this church. I'm a primary teacher during the week but on Sundays I say hello to people as they come in to church. I make sure new people are introduced to some Christians who come regularly, to make them feel welcome.

I am also on the Street Team. Two evenings a week I work with supporting the homeless. I do this by cooking food some weeks and other weeks by going out into the town to take soup and sandwiches to people in need. I think being a Christian is about being like Jesus to everyone around me.

Hi, I'm Naomi and I lead the worship at this church. This means that I organise the music, and sometimes lead the band in services. I sing and play guitar. I try to help people remember that we are here to worship God, because God is so great! We praise and thank God for all the great things God has done.

Worship is not just about singing, though. It is about following God in everything we do. We ask Jesus for forgiveness, and we say thank you to him for taking away the bad things we do. Jesus also shows us how to live, by loving other people and doing what we can to help those in need.

Hi, I'm Tim. I'm pastor of this Baptist church. I'm called a pastor because my job is to be like a shepherd to the Christians who come to church, but also to help people in the wider community.

I try to guide people in how to live well, teaching them about Jesus and God, using the Bible. I visit people in hospital when they are ill, and also in their homes when they are well. I love bringing God's love to people's everyday lives. I try to pray for all my congregation, including the children. I work with a group of deacons. They are members of the church who give their time to serve and lead others.

As-salaam aleikum! I am Wasim and I am the imam at this mosque. My job is most importantly to lead people in the five daily prayers. I stand at the front and help Muslims to submit to Allah by praying together. At Friday prayers I give a short sermon or khutba.

During the rest of the week I help people when they are looking for advice on spiritual or practical matters, to bring them closer to Allah. I visit people who are sick. I also perform wedding ceremonies – but not as often as I would like!

Hello, I am Imran. At this mosque I am a hafiz. This means that I have spent many hours learning to memorise the words of Allah, the Holy Qur'an. This helps me to be closer to Allah because I have his words in my head all the time.

I help to lead the madrassah, the mosque school. I help children and young people to learn Arabic so that they can read the Holy Qur'an. Some of my students are learning to become Hafiz too!

At this mosque we run youth groups. We want to help young people get fit and healthy, but also to respect others.

Hello, I am Nasima and I sometimes worship at the mosque, particularly at Friday prayers. I sit in the balcony with my daughter, Abidah.

I help at the madrassah twice a week, with the younger children, aged 6–8.

I am a lawyer in my day job and so the mosque committee have asked if I can give advice to people who need help. I might advise on buying a home, but I also offer advice to women who want help on a whole range of issues.

Learning from six teachings from the Bible and the Qur'an (W)

Whenever two or three are gathered together in my name, said Jesus, I will be with them.

Matthew 18:19-21

Wherever the hour of prayer overtakes you, you shall perform it. That place is a mosque.

Hadith

Love the Lord your God with all your heart, soul, mind and strength, and love your neighbour as you love yourself.

Matthew 22:37-39

God's mosques should only be tended by one who believes in God and the Last Day, and is constant in prayer, and gives Zakat [charity], and stands in awe of none but God: for only such a person may hope to be among the rightly-guided!

Qur'an 9:18

Be filled with the Spirit, speaking to one another with psalms, hymns, and songs from the Spirit. Sing and make music from your heart to the Lord, always giving thanks to God the Father for everything, in the name of our Lord Jesus Christ.

Ephesians 5:19-20

In houses [of worship] which Allah has permitted to be built so that His name may be remembered in them; there glorify Him in the mornings and the evenings.

Qur'an 24:36

What is important about the places of worship where we live?

Background knowledge for teachers

This unit is set out as an enquiry that will fit well with work that schools may be doing on their local area within Geography and History. The unit shows how pupils can engage in good RE learning while engaging in a cross-curricular unit of work.

The photographs in this unit are there both as a stimulus and to act as a comparison to the evidence of religion you may find in your local area, allowing pupils to consider similarity and difference, a key RE skill.

Within this unit of work pupils will need to go out on a walk in the area around the school to take photos of evidence of religion in their neighbourhood. As part of this learning pupils should, if practical, visit a local place of worship and meet some of the people who belong to the religious community. This type of Learning Outside the Classroom is memorable to pupils.

The unit culminates with a real-life task creating a noticeboard or web page for a local place of worship, showing what they do for their members and the wider community.

Essential knowledge for pupils

Pupils should know:

- how religion has affected and is in evidence in their local community
- that members of most religious communities believe that they should provide support and resources for the wider community.

Links across the curriculum

Geography:

- use fieldwork to observe, measure and record the human and physical features in the local area, using a range of methods, including sketch maps, plans and graphs, and digital technologies.

Moral and Cultural Development:

- understand what a local place of worship offers to the local community and why the people who belong to the place of worship want to support the wider community
- understand the effect that religion has and has had in the local community.

Assessment for Learning

The following pupil-friendly 'I can' statements describe the learning that may be expected of pupils in the 7–9 age range:

Level	Description of achievement: I can ...
2 Almost all pupils in this age group	- **identify** examples of religion in my locality - **give two simple reasons** why religious believers like to go to their place of worship - *recognise the values shown by the local place of worship as they provide resources for the wider community.*
3 Many pupils in this age group	- **describe** the significance of a place of worship in the local community - **make a link between** a piece of sacred text and an example of religion in evidence in my local community - *suggest answers to questions local religious believers might give about providing charity and resources for the wider community.*
4 The most able pupils in this age group	- **describe the impact** that religion has had on my local community and compare that with a different community - *show understanding of how a local place of worship has connected up teaching from sacred text with their actions in the local community compare this to an example from a different locality.*

This unit helps pupils in Scotland to achieve RME 1-01b, 1-09c and 2-09d.

Web support

The following resources are available for download by RE Today subscribers:

- The photographs of religion in the neighbourhood on pp.22-3.

This activity enables you to assess the prior knowledge that your pupils have about religious buildings and religious activity in general and in the area that they live.

Ask the pupils to:

- **identify** as many examples of religious buildings as they can, including places of worship, but also other related buildings e.g. cemetery, vicarage, etc.
- **categorise** the buildings into different religions. Ensure all pupils are aware of the correct names for the different places of worship.

Introduce the evidence of religion around us (photographs on pp.22-3). Explain that all these photos were taken in Leicester. Ask the children to work in groups of four. Give each group two contrasting pictures, each one stuck in the middle of a large piece of paper.

Ask each group to:

- write what they can work out from the photo in black. For example, which religion this is, where they think this might be found, what it is, why it is there.
- write what they need to know about the photo in red. For example; who was St John? Why is Christ being called a king? Why are Muslims raising money? What is Mahatma Gandhi House? Why does the Catholic church have a school?
- research, as a group, some more about their pictures. Use the internet to search out more information.
- write a description of one of their pictures, showing what it represents. The description should show the significance of that building or person or object to a community.

Look at the pictures as a whole class. What difference does religion make in this place? How do you know?

Discuss with the children the historical influence of religion, e.g. war memorials and street names.

Discuss the difference religion, and the people from places of worship, make now, e.g. raising money at Ramadan, Mahatma Gandhi house (an old people's home), church groups running preschools and other services for the community.

Activity 2 Walking your patch

Take the pupils out to walk round an area in a community near your school.

- What evidence can they find of religion?

Take a camera and ask the pupils to take pictures of evidence of religion in the area, e.g. place names, noticeboards, places of worship.

End your walk at a local place of worship. Arrange for a leader or member of the religious group to be there to talk to the children about what is done for people in the place of worship and for people in the local community. Set the pupils up to ask questions of the speaker, such as why they do what they do.

If the nearest place of worship is too far away to include in your walk, visit yourself and collect evidence of what the people from that community do to support their member and the wider community, e.g. lunch clubs, youth club, money advice or employment advice. See the examples below.

See: http://trinitycheltenham.com/
See: www.npls.org.uk/

Additionally you might ask pupils to look for evidence as a piece of homework, encouraging them to look in food shops and for symbols in cars or houses. Pupils may have opportunity to take pictures or tell you about religion in a community further afield.

Activity 3 Similar and different

Compare the pictures that you have taken with the ones that were taken in Leicester.

- What is similar and what is different about the evidence that you have collected from each community?
- What influence does religion have on each community?

Introduce the quotes from sacred text on p.24.

- Do any of these link to the photographs?
- How do they link?
- How are people from the different religions following this advice?

1 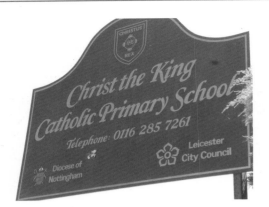	**2** 
3 	**4** 
5 	**6** 

This information is for you to share with pupils when you think it will support their enquiry. They may not need this information or these questions.

Picture 1

Many primary and secondary schools are supported by different religions. Are there any in your area? Why do you think religions are involved in educating people?

Picture 2

Often streets are named after significant religious figures. Who was St John? Are there any streets in your area named after significant religious figures?

Picture 3

This writing is in Hebrew over the Orthodox synagogue in Leicester. Is there evidence of different languages and religions in your area?

Picture 4

This was a poster used in Ramadan 2013 to raise money for Islamic Aid. During Ramadan and Eid a large amount of money is raised for charitable causes. Are there any posters about religions raising money in your area?

Picture 5

Mahatma Gandhi house is a residential home for old people in Leicester. Why do you think a home for old people might be named after this inspirational Hindu figure?

Picture 6

Road signs show the influence that religious figures and buildings have had in an area. What can you find in your area?

Photocopiable by purchasing institutions

RE Today Services

7

8

9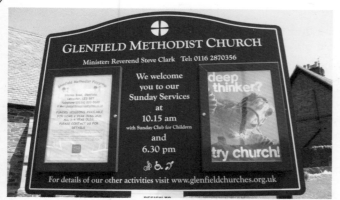

10

11

12

This information is for you to share with pupils when you think it will support their enquiry. They may not need this information or these questions.

Picture 7
The local village war memorial has a cross on the top. Is there a memorial in your area. Does it have any symbols on it? Why do you think this is?

Picture 8
Often religious buildings have quotes from sacred text. Why? This one says 'The best of all is God is with us'

Picture 9
Outside most places of worship there is a name board that suggests some of the things that happen inside. What is advertised on the name boards outside places of worship in your area?

Picture 10
An Islamic star and crescent appear on the gate outside a local mosque. Why do religious buildings use symbols as well as words?

Picture 11
In the local churchyard there are many gravestones that have a cross on them. Why do you think this is? Is this the same in your area?

Picture 12
This murti of Ganesh, a Hindu deity, is on an ordinary windowsill in a house. Why do you think it is there? What other religious artefacts or symbols can you see in your area?

What difference have places of worship made in our area?

Set the pupils a real or imagined challenge. The local place of worship is planning to redesign the noticeboards inside and outside their building. They would like your pupils to come up with a series of items to display that show the local community what goes on both for the members of the place of worship and for the members of the community. They also want people to understand why they do what they do. Ask the pupils to work in groups to create something for the noticeboards or for the place of worship's website.

They might create:

- a map of the local area with the place of worship in the centre and strings stretching to different people the community is helping. Each of the strings could lead to a quote about something the place of worship is doing.
- a series of pictures of events organised by the place of worship with lift-up flaps – under the flaps could be event details and a quote from someone about the event
- a leaflet to be given out in the local library.

Whatever the pupils create it must explain what the community does for its members, for the wider community, and refer to a piece of sacred text to explain why the people from this place of worship behave in this way.

Be the change you want to see in the world. *Mahatma Gandhi* *Hinduism*	All people are responsible for one another. *Jewish Talmud Sanhedrin 27b* *Judaism*
Have compassion on those who live on earth and he who is in heaven will have compassion on you. *The Prophet Mohammed* *Islam*	Love the Lord your God with all your heart, all your soul and all your strength. Love your neighbour as yourself. *Deuteronomy 6:5, Leviticus 19:18* *Judaism and Christianity*
Whenever you see someone else hungry or thirsty or a stranger or sick or in prison and do not look after them you do not look after me. *Matthew 25:35-36* *Christianity*	A man once asked the prophet what was the best thing in Islam, and the latter replied: 'It is to feed the hungry and to give the greeting of peace both to those you know and to those you do not know.' *Hadith of Bukhari* *Islam*

Five daily duties (Pancha Maha Yagnas)

1 Worship God at the home shrine or at the mandir, using ritual, prayer or meditations
2 Study the scriptures
3 Contemplate teachings of the wise and the actions and words of elders and ancestors
4 Provide food for human beings or animals who are in need
5 Serve guests with love, respect and reverence.

Hinduism

Photocopiable by purchasing institutions

RE Today Services

Shall we sell the church?

Background knowledge for teachers

Church buildings are key features of the UK skyline. We pass them every day as we go about our business; sometimes we go inside, for worship, as a visitor, or for the wedding or funeral of someone we know. Along with the places of worship of other faiths, churches are important landmarks in our communities.

This section enables pupils to engage with the question of what happens when a congregation can no longer pay for the upkeep of a church building and has to make hard decisions about its future – decisions which are consistent with the teachings of the Bible and which recognise that the work of *the* church can, and perhaps should, continue in other ways.

There are some key concepts and vocabulary that is important to understand yourself and share with your pupils.

Church

- A church is a place where Christians meet to worship God.
- *The* Church is the worldwide community of Christians. There are approximately 2.2 billion Christians in the world today (out of a world population of 7 billion); Christianity is the world's largest religion.

Stewardship

- The responsibility to look after what belongs to someone else on their behalf.
- Christians believe that God created the world and gave human beings a special responsibility within Creation to cultivate it, guard it and use it wisely and justly (Bible: Genesis 1:28; Genesis 2:15; Genesis 9:3; Psalm 24:1).

Assessment for Learning

This section shows some of the outcomes achievable by pupils of different abilities in the 9–11 age range.

Level	Description of achievement: I can ...
3 Almost all pupils in this age group	• **make a link between** what Jesus taught and how some Christians think they should use their wealth • *ask some questions* about why Christians try to help other people.
4 Many pupils in this age group	• **make a link between** Christian beliefs and how some Christians behave • *ask questions and suggest answers* as to why Christians should consider the needs of others.
5 The most able pupils in this age group	• **explain** how some Christian teaching would inspire Christians to put their faith into action. • *express my own views* on the value of Christians engaging in serving others.

This unit helps pupils in Scotland to achieve RME 2-01b, 2-01c and 2-02b.

Essential knowledge for pupils

Pupils should know:

- A church is a building, a place of worship. *The* Church is the worldwide community of 2.2 billion Christians.
- Churches of all denominations are funded by money given by their members; they receive no money from the government.
- Christians believe that they must be good stewards of everything they have, including their church buildings.
- Church buildings sometimes become disused or redundant (no longer needed for worship). They are sold/and or converted for other use.

Links across the curriculum

Enquiry skills
- interpretation, evaluation, reflection and application

English
- increasing ability to manipulate elements of writing to persuade others

SMSC
- increasing ability to reflect on the impact of faith in peoples' lives.

RE Today
Services

25

Activity 1 — Introduction

This activity is an important introduction to Activity 2. It introduces key concepts and ideas, provides information and opens up discussion about alternative uses of church buildings, and encourages connections between Christian teaching and the church's use of resources.

Ask pupils to:

- **identify** as many examples as they can of church buildings which have been converted into something else, e.g. community centre, warehouse, art centre, place of worship for another religion, offices.

- **consider** the range of uses for former or redundant churches, using those they have found (above) and the resources on pp.28-9. Are some uses more acceptable than others?

- **suggest** how (a) the congregation of these churches and (b) the pupils themselves feel about this change of use. What reasons can they give for their thoughts?

- **identify** the reasons given for and against a disused church being converted into a theatre (Resource 1, p.28). What reasons for and against might the congregation of the church have given before they decided to sell?

- **connect** the Christian idea of stewardship with the conversion and/or sale of a church to another use. Consider Resources 2, 6 and 8 on pp. 28–9. How might the sale or conversion of a church be an example of good stewardship?

- **suggest** how *the* Church can continue and grow if *a* church is disused and is converted into something else.

Move on to Activity 2.

Activity 2 — Enquiry: should the church be sold?

This activity provides an opportunity for pupils to work collaboratively to investigate and apply the information and thinking covered in Activity 1 to a real situation, to justify an opinion with clear reference to Christian teaching and to reflect on outcomes.

Ask pupils to:

- **work in small groups** to investigate the options facing St Mark's Church and decide which in their view is the best option for the church. Their recommendation should be:
  o financially viable
  o achievable (realistic)
  o consistent with Christian teaching, e.g. on stewardship.

- **use** the following resources to inform their investigation: a copy of the 'Background information' resource (p.27); the use of church buildings resource (pp.28–9); one of the Task Group cards (p.30).

- **decide** which members of their group should make the presentation to the panel, and work together as a group to **create** the presentation. Pupils can choose the format of this presentation, e.g. notes on cards, PowerPoint. It should be persuasive, draw on the facts of the situation facing St Mark's, and show how their group's recommendation is consistent with Christian teaching.

- **present** their recommendation to the panel, which might consist of: pupils from another class; members of the school staff or governors; members of the local Christian faith community; or members of the class. The panel should be required to justify its final decision in terms of how it meets the criteria above.

- **write** an individual evaluative response to the final decision. They should use the following starter and make sure they refer to Christian religious teaching in their answer.

This is the correct decision for the Christian community because ...

Others might disagree with this decision because ...

RE Today
Services

Where is St Mark's?

St Mark's Church was built in 1924 in what was then a village, and is now a small town.

It is one of three churches in the area; there is also a mosque and a gurdwara.

The area consists of:

- houses (social housing and owner occupied)
- shopping centre including several large supermarkets
- three pubs
- several small factories
- two primary schools and a secondary school
- a medical centre
- a local football club.

How is the building used?

- **Services:** There are two services on a Sunday – at 10am and 6pm. Wedding and funeral services take place occasionally.
- **Choir:** Choir practice takes place on Friday evenings.
- **Meetings:** A small room at the back of the church is used during the week for church meetings.
- **School:** The local primary schools visit the church as part of their RE lessons and for annual Christmas carol concerts. Teachers of one school use the car park during the week.

Who attends St Marks?
Today

- On most Sundays 30–40 people attend the 10am service, and 5–10 attend the 6pm service.
- Most members of the church are aged 60+ and are retired. There are several young families with children.

Ten years ago

- There were 150+ people at the 10am service. Most of the congregation were aged 30–60 years and in work. There were 15 young people under 16 years.

How much money does the church have?
Income (per year)

Collections: £18,000

Donations: £10,000

Interest on savings: £100

Expenditure (per year)

Minister's salary: £25,000

Gas, electricity and water: £3,000

Organist: £2,000

Youth worker: £2,000

Repairs: £2,000

Materials: £2,000

Savings

£50,000

The church owns the building and its contents, and the land.

What state is the building in?

The building is in a reasonably good condition.

Ten years ago the church had a major fundraising campaign and was able to replace the roof, repair the heating system, install new lighting and a public address system, and paint the inside of the church.

The land around the church is mainly grass, with a small area tarmacked for car parking.

Who works at St Marks?

- **Revd Gill Humphreys** has been at the church for six years but is looking for a new job as she knows the church will be unable to afford her salary next year. She is unlikely to be replaced.
- **Dave Jackson** is the organist and choir master.
- **Sarah Porter** works with the children and young people.
Members of the church volunteer to tidy the church grounds and clean the inside.

Resource 1

RESIDENTS' FEARS OVER WORKINGTON CHURCH CONVERSION

By Jenny Barwise

People living near to a disused church earmarked to be transformed into a theatre have raised concerns about the development.

Publican Paul Scott, who owns The Vine Bar and The Grapes at Workington, has applied for planning permission to change the empty Trinity Methodist Church into a theatre and arts and craft centre.

A consultation into the plans was launched when the plans were submitted to Allerdale Council last month and the News & Star can now reveal the outcome.

Amanda Marshall, of Wybrow Terrace, objected to the plans. She said that during performances at the theatre the public will 'undoubtedly' want to exit the premises and will lead to groups of people standing around outside.

'Due to consumption of alcohol there could be raised voices causing a disturbance in an otherwise residential area,' she added. She also has concerns with parking and increased traffic.

Another objector, Sean Mccarron, said that there was 'no need' for the theatre as there is already a suitable place for 'this type of entertainment' at the Carnegie Theatre on Finkle Street.

And John Metherell who lives on the same street said that he has taken advice from a local land agent regarding the value of his property and has been advised that it would be devalued by up to 10 per cent.

'Basically, what it means is that a row of Georgian terraced houses in a very desirable location which currently sell very quickly will become almost impossible to sell.'

Cumbria County Council's historic environment officer, Jeremy Parsons, said that records indicate the church was designed in 1890 and is one of the 'grandest Non-conformist churches in the county.'

He added: 'Any sympathetic scheme that maintains a viable use for the building would be supported, and while the exterior of the building will virtually stay the same in the proposed conversion, the interior will be impacted upon.'

He has recommended that an archaeological building recording programme be undertaken.

If the proposals are given the go-ahead, about 50 people would be employed. Trinity Church is near the Carnegie Theatre, but Mr Scott insisted his arts centre would not be in direct competition with it or the Theatre Royal in Washington Street.

Cumberland *News & Star*, Saturday 13 April 2013

www.newsandstar.co.uk

Resource 2

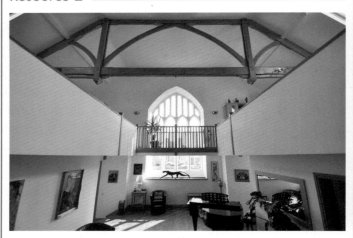

The Old Church, Horncliffe, provides five- star bed & breakfast accommodation in a converted church.
See: www.oldchurchhorncliffe.co.uk

Resource 3

Share your food with the hungry and open your homes to the homeless poor. Give clothes to those who have nothing to wear, and do not refuse to help your own relatives.

Bible, Isaiah 58:7

Resource 4

Riverside Church in Birmingham meets in a local high school each Sunday.
See: www.riverside-church.org.uk

Photocopiable by purchasing institutions

RE Today Services

Resource 5

Jesus said:

Don't store up treasures on earth! Moths and rust can destroy them, and thieves can break in and steal them. Instead, store up your treasures in heaven, where moths and rust cannot destroy them, and thieves cannot break in and steal them. Your heart will always be where your treasure is.

Bible, Matthew 6:19–21

Resource 7

Jesus said:

The love of money causes all kinds of trouble.

Bible, 1 Timothy, 6:10

Resource 9

A Rich Young Man

A rich man asked Jesus what he must to do gain eternal life. He was already obeying all the commandments.

Jesus said:

'If you want to be perfect, go and sell everything you own. Give the money to the poor, and you will have riches in heaven.'

Bible, Matthew 19:21

Resource 10

About the first Christians

'The group of followers all felt the same way about everything. None of them claimed that their possessions were their own, and they shared everything they had with each other.'

Bible, Acts 4: 32

Resource 6

St Basil's works across the West Midlands with young people aged 16-25 who are homeless or at risk of homelessness, helping over 4,500 young people per year. It was converted into a centre for working with the homeless in 1972.

See: www.stbasils.org.uk

Resource 8

The Church is a café, bar, and restaurant and club in a converted church in Dublin.

See: www.thechurch.ie

Task Group 1: Sell St Mark's to a developer!

Background

- St Mark's Church no longer has the money to carry on and has to decide what it should do. It has received an offer from a developer who would demolish the church and build social housing on the land.

Your task

- Investigate the offer from the developer and present your recommendation, with reasons, to the committee which will make the final decision. You will need the 'Background information' resource sheet.

Questions to consider:

- What are the main arguments for and against selling St Mark's to the developer?
- What should St Mark's do with the proceeds for the sale of the church?
- What would happen to the congregation?
- How would selling the land enable St Mark's to put Jesus' teachings into practice?

Task Group 2: Keep St Mark's and change how the building is used!

Background

- St Mark's Church no longer has the money to carry on and has to decide what it should do. It is considering changing how the building is used in order to generate income.

Your task

- Investigate using St Mark's in different ways and present your recommendation, with reasons, to the committee which will make the final decision. You will need the 'Background information' resource sheet.

Questions to consider:

- What alternative uses for St Mark's can you think of? e.g. craft centre, community centre, café, art centre, conference centre.
- What are the main arguments for and against changing the way the church is used?
- What would happen to the congregation? For example, could it continue to meet in part of the building?
- How would changing the use of St Mark's enable the church to put Jesus' teachings into practice?

Task Group 3: Keep St Mark's and join forces with another church!

Background

- St Mark's Church no longer has the money to carry on and has to decide what it should do. Nearby Clifton Community Church is struggling with a poor building; St Mark's is considering joining forces with Clifton.

Your task

- Investigate the suggestion of joining forces with Clifton and present your recommendation, with reasons, to the committee which will make the final decision. You will need the 'Background information' resource sheet.

Questions to consider:

- What are the main arguments for and against joining forces with another church?
- How would St Mark's ensure it had the finances to continue?
- How would the two congregations, and the two ministers, work together?
- How would joining with another church put Jesus' teachings into practice?

Photocopiable by purchasing institutions

RE Today Services

Subject Leader support: visiting places of worship

Why visit places of worship?

Visits to places of worship can really help bring a religion to life for pupils, and are well worth the hard work required to organise them. Learning outside the classroom is often more meaningful to pupils and is remembered for far longer, enabling them to connect the experiences to other parts of their learning.

Visits can:

- enrich the learning process. They are far more effective than learning only from texts and electronic sources; the atmosphere in a place of worship cannot be simulated in a classroom

- provide opportunities to meet people of faith in their community setting and to engage in dialogue with them

- provide opportunities to experience the sacred in an appropriate setting. Many artefacts and some holy scriptures can only be seen in the place where they are used.

- contribute to the self-esteem of pupils whose place of worship is being visited and facilitate school and community links

- extend pupils' knowledge, understanding and experience of the world of which religion is an important factor

- be part of a planned curriculum, and integral to the learning that will take place; a visit would contribute hugely to pupils' progress and understanding. Visits are never about indoctrination or persuading pupils to agree with the beliefs of the religion being studied.

- provide opportunities for cross-curricular learning. Many aspects of the school curriculum can be studied through a religious building, e.g. the arts, literacy, history, mathematics and design.

How should I prepare for a visit?

It is important to:

- make contact *beforehand* with your hosts and all concerned with the visit

- discuss with your hosts what pupils will see and what they will participate in, and prepare your pupils so that they know what to do, e.g. whether to observe or take part

- make careful preparation regarding appropriate behaviour, dress and purposes of the visit to help make the visit a successful learning experience

- make available – in suitable format for the age groups – background materials on people, culture, religion, and uses of the place of worship. This will help them gain a deeper understanding of its purpose.

- prepare questions and tasks to direct pupils' attention to some features, and to evoke use of all senses, awareness of atmosphere and their emotional responses. Visits should not just be about acquiring facts.

- include multi-sensory work, exploration, enquiry, teamwork and some open-ended questions: these help make quality activities

- arrange a talk by a visitor from the community whose place of worship is being visited. Brief them clearly; it cannot be assumed that members of faith communities are skilled in talking to children

- find out in advance if it is possible to make sketches, take photographs or videos, etc

- ensure that the person who will take you around the place of worship is aware of the purpose and theme of your visit so the talk to the children can have a specific focus

- reassure pupils and any adults accompanying them that they will not be obliged to do anything they do not wish to on the visit

- remind pupils that eating, chewing gum and drinking are not allowed. However, in mandirs food may be offered as part of the experience.

- be aware that strong and vivid imagery may be encountered during some visits.

What is the dress code?

Temple (Buddhism)

- No head covering is usually required.
- Preferably wear tops with long sleeves.
- Shoes will need to be removed before entering the building.

Church (Christianity)

- There is generally no particular dress code for visiting a church; however some churches would expect shoulders to be covered.
- Traditionally men and boys would uncover their heads.

Gurdwara (Sikhism)

- Visitors will be expected to cover their heads and remove their shoes.

Mandir (Hinduism)

- Visitors should dress modestly, avoiding shorts, short skirts, bare arms or tight-fitting clothes.
- Shoes will need to be removed before entering the prayer hall.

Mosque (Islam)

- Visitors should dress modestly, preferably wearing trousers or mid-calf-length skirts. Clothes should not be tight-fitting or revealing and arms should be covered.
- Visitors should cover their heads.
- On entry to the mosque, shoes will need to be removed.

Synagogue (Judaism)

- Visitors should dress modestly, avoiding shorts, short skirts, bare arms or tight-fitting clothes.
- Men should cover their heads.
- In orthodox synagogues, married women are required to wear head coverings.

How can I engage parents?

Most parents welcome the opportunity for their children to visit places of worship. However, occasionally some parents will object to visits to some places of worship. Reasons can vary and may include the cost of the trip as well as religious and, sometimes, racist objections.

Schools are recommended always to ask parents to explain their decision, while remembering that parents have the right to withdraw their children from some or all of RE on grounds of conscience.

Ways to engage all parents include:

- having a clear policy on which parents and pupils have been consulted, which has been ratified by the governing body and is supported by all members of the school community. This can be incorporated into the race equality policy or the RE policy.
- inviting parents to attend trips to places of worship as helpers
- using parents' evenings, assemblies, displays and newsletters to promote understanding of religious and cultural diversity and of previous visits to places of worship
- being unequivocal in the school's approach to racism, stereotyping and prejudice
- working with the local community to raise awareness, e.g. the local church supporting the visit to the mosque
- having a period of preparation for the visit so that pupils' interest and enthusiasm are high
- stressing the purpose of the visit to parents, some of whom might have an incorrect view of what will happen – such as expecting participation in others' worship.

Web support

RE:ONLINE

www.reonline.org.uk/specials/places-of-worship

CLEO

www.cleo.net.uk

Engaging with faith communities

www.ewfc.co.uk

RE Today
Services